WORKBOOK

FOR 50 SEL LESSONS VOL. 1

David Paris

INTRODUCTION

The *Workbook for 50 Social Emotional Lessons Vol. 1* is a great tool to capture the SEL magic that awaits your classroom. The workbook is a container and incubator for all the crucial lessons from *50 Social Emotional Learning Lessons Vol. 1*. Social emotional learning blossoms when you articulate your experience into words and these words have a home in this workbook.

There are 50 worksheets that will help improve retention, increase accountability, and promote self-expression and visibility. Homework trackers are included at the end of every Lesson for practice and to document the impact these skills have on students' social emotional lives. Assessments at the end of every unit provide reflection and evaluation.

Your classroom and students will be forever transformed by this curriculum. *Workbook for 50 Social Emotional Lessons Vol. 1* will document the journey.

UNIT 1: Community Building

LESSON 1: CLASSROOM AGREEMENTS

ACTIVITY 1: OPENING QUESTION

1. What is the story behind your name?

....

....

2. A classmate's story I found interesting was ....

....

....

ACTIVITY 2: TINY TEACH

1. What I taught ....

....

2. What I learned ....

....

3. What I learned about teaching and learning

....

....

....

ACTIVITY 3: GROUP AGREEMENTS

1. Which agreement was most important to you and why?

....

....

....

ACTIVITY 4: ARE YOU LIKE THIS OR LIKE THAT?

1. What answers did you choose that best represented what you are like?

....

....

....

2. Which answers among your classmates interested you? Why?

....

....

....

HOMEWORK

Notice your relationships to the classroom agreements.

HOMEWORK TRACKER

Something I did in class

....

....

....

Classroom agreement

....

....

....

How I felt afterwards

....

....

....

LESSON 2: GETTING TO KNOW EACH OTHER

ACTIVITY 1: OPENING QUESTION

1. If you could travel backward or forward in time, when and where would you want to go?

....

....

2. What is a classmate's answer that you found interesting?

....

....

ACTIVITY 2: MOVE YOUR BUTT IF...

1. What was it like to share a commonality with someone else?

....

....

2. What was it like to be different from the group?

....

....

....

ACTIVITY 3: WHO WROTE THAT?

1. What was something interesting that you enjoyed sharing about yourself?

....

....

....

2. What was something interesting you learned about other members of the class?

....

....

....

ACTIVITY 4: IF I WERE A...

1. What were you able to share about yourself through the questions?

....

....

....

2. Did anyone's answer surprise you?

....

....

HOMEWORK

Consider asking a follow up question to anything you've learned about another student.

HOMEWORK TRACKER

A question you asked a classmate

....

....

....

....

Your classmate's answer

....

....

....

....

LESSON 3: LEARNING ABOUT WHO WE ARE

ACTIVITY 1: OPENING QUESTION

1. How many siblings do you have or are you an only child?

....

....

....

ACTIVITY 2: HUMAN TREASURE HUNT

1. What did you learn about your classmates?

....

....

....

2. What do you still want to learn about your classmates?

....

....

....

....

ACTIVITY 3: Tracing Who We Are

1. What memories did you share?

....

....

....

2. What is something interesting that you learned about someone else in the class?

....

....

ACTIVITY 4: Web of Stories

1. How does the yarn reflect the connection people have with each other?

....

....

....

HOMEWORK

Notice how you feel now compared to how you felt before the first Lesson.

HOMEWORK TRACKER

Something you learned about a classmate

....

....

....

....

....

Something a classmate learned about you

....

....

....

....

....

LESSON 4: GROUP VALUES

ACTIVITY 1: OPENING QUESTIONS

1. What value is most important to you?

....

....

2. When have you experienced your value in your life?

....

....

ACTIVITY 2: INDIVIDUAL VALUES

1. What value did you share with the class?

....

....

....

2. How did it feel to connect to your value?

....

....

ACTIVITY 3: Sounds of the Universe

1. What did it feel like to collectively help a classmate?

....

....

....

ACTIVITY 4: Class Value

1. What is one value that resonates with you after today's lesson and why is it important to you?

....

....

2. What are your top five values for a class to be an effective learning environment?

....

....

HOMEWORK

Notice when classmates demonstrate the chosen class values.

HOMEWORK TRACKER

Something you did

....

....

....

....

....

Corresponding individual value

....

....

....

....

....

LESSON 5: INTEGRATING VALUES

ACTIVITY 1: OPENING QUESTION

1. How has the class demonstrated the class values since the last time you met?

....

....

....

ACTIVITY 2: GROUP JUGGLING

1. What can this activity teach us about how to support each other as a group?

....

....

....

2. During the activity, what did you do to help someone else?

....

....

....

ACTIVITY 3: SILENT LINE-UP

1. What did this activity teach you about creativity?

....

....

2. How did your group work together?

....

....

ACTIVITY 4: ACRONYM PARTY

1. What was your process for creating acronyms?

....

....

2. How did your group use teamwork?

....

....

HOMEWORK

Notice how students work together in groups.

HOMEWORK TRACKER

Something that happened in the class

....

....

....

....

....

Corresponding classroom value

....

....

....

....

....

LESSON 6: MEANING

ACTIVITY 1: OPENING QUESTION

1. What is your favorite spot at home or in your neighborhood and why?

....

....

....

ACTIVITY 2: BIN OF MEANING

1. How did you feel sharing what was meaningful for you?

....

....

....

2. What was it like to hear about what was meaningful for others?

....

....

....

ACTIVITY 3: COMMUNITY MURAL

1. What were you able to contribute to the group?

....

....

....

....

2. What are the advantages and disadvantages of doing art as a group?

....

....

....

....

HOMEWORK

Think about what rituals you have in your life that are meaningful to you.

HOMEWORK TRACKER

Something that is meaningful to you

....

....

....

....

....

Why is it meaningful to you?

....

....

....

....

....

UNIT 1: POST-ASSESSMENT

To what extent do you agree with each statement?

1. I feel more connected to my class than at the beginning of this community building unit.

☐ *Strongly Disagree* ☐ *Disagree* ☐ *Agree* ☐ *Strongly Agree*

2. I feel more supported by classmates than at the beginning of this community building unit.

☐ *Strongly Disagree* ☐ *Disagree* ☐ *Agree* ☐ *Strongly Agree*

3. I feel more connected to my values than at the beginning of this community building unit.

☐ *Strongly Disagree* ☐ *Disagree* ☐ *Agree* ☐ *Strongly Agree*

Complete the prompt:

4. What I learned in this community building unit that will help me in school:

....

....

....

....

....

5. What I learned in this community building unit that will help me in life:

....

....

....

....

....

6. What I still want to learn or experience:

....

....

....

....

....

UNIT 2: Active Listening

LESSON 7: LISTENING BASICS

ACTIVITY 1: OPENING QUESTION

1. How do you know when someone is listening to you well or is not listening well?

....

....

....

....

ACTIVITY 2: LOOKS / SOUNDS / FEELS LIKE

1. In what ways do you need to improve your listening skills?

....

....

....

....

....

....

....

ACTIVITY 3: CONCENTRIC CIRCLES

1. How do you feel after being listened to
by so many of your peers?

....

....

....

....

HOMEWORK

Notice when you or others are listening well and when you and others are not.

HOMEWORK TRACKER

Who did you listen to?

....

....

....

....

What did you do to demonstrate good listening skills?

....

....

....

....

....

....

What happened afterwards?

....

....

....

....

....

....

LESSON 8: OPEN-ENDED QUESTIONS

ACTIVITY 1: OPENING QUESTION

1. Who listens to you well?

....

....

....

ACTIVITY 2: DOG AND BONE

1. What techniques did the bone thieves use to stay quiet?

....

....

....

....

2. What did you learn about listening?

....

....

....

ACTIVITY 3: ASKING QUESTIONS

1. How does asking questions affect a conversation?

....

....

....

....

ACTIVITY 4: WALK AND TALK

1. What did you learn about the relationship between good listening and asking questions?

....

....

....

....

....

HOMEWORK

Practice asking questions when listening to someone.

HOMEWORK TRACKER

Who did you listen to?

....

....

....

What question did you ask?

....

....

....

What was the result?

....

....

....

LESSON 9: LISTENING RESPONSES

ACTIVITY 1: OPENING QUESTION

1. How do you like people to respond after you say something?

....

....

....

....

ACTIVITY 2: THE ART OF THE RESPONSE

1. What is your favorite way to respond to people after someone tells you something?

....

....

....

....

ACTIVITY 3: GROUP CONVERSATIONS

1. How did responses differ in a group?

....

....

....

....

HOMEWORK

Notice how you and others respond that demonstrates poor or good listening skills.

HOMEWORK TRACKER

Who did you listen to?

....

....

....

....

How did you respond?

....

....

....

....

....

....

What happened afterwards?

....

....

....

....

....

....

LESSON 10: PARAPHRASING

ACTIVITY 1: OPENING QUESTION

1. When has miscommunication been a problem in your life?

....

....

ACTIVITY 2: BACK-TO-BACK DRAWING

1. Did your drawings look like what was described?

....

....

2. What was difficult about describing the image?
About listening?

....

....

....

3. What did you learn about communication?

....

....

ACTIVITY 3: PARAPHRASE PRACTICE

1. How did paraphrasing improve communication?

....

....

....

....

ACTIVITY 4: COMMUNICATION BREAKDOWN

1. How does paraphrasing compare with communicating without paraphrasing?

....

....

....

....

HOMEWORK

Paraphrase what someone says to make sure you understand them.

HOMEWORK TRACKER

Who did you paraphrase?

....

....

....

What words did you use?

....

....

....

What were the results?

....

....

....

LESSON 11: PARAPHRASING WITH TONE

ACTIVITY 1: OPENING QUESTION

1. What tone of voice gets your attention?

....

....

ACTIVITY 2: BLAH, BLAH, BLAH

1. What were you able and unable to communicate?

....

....

....

....

2. How did your body language and tone affect comprehension?

....

....

....

....

ACTIVITY 3: PARAPHRASE PRACTICE WITH TONE

1. How did listening to tone affect your feeling of being heard?

....

....

....

....

HOMEWORK

Practice paraphrasing while matching someone's tone.

HOMEWORK TRACKER

Who did you paraphrase?

....

....

....

....

What words did you use for paraphrase?

....

....

....

....

What tone did you use?

....

....

....

....

What happened afterwards?

....

....

....

....

LESSON 12: LISTENING AND DISAGREEMENT

ACTIVITY 1: OPENING QUESTION

1. What do you do when you disagree with someone?

....

....

....

....

ACTIVITY 2: SHARING UNDERSTANDING IN DISAGREEMENT

1. Were you able to communicate your perspective?

....

....

....

2. Did you understand the arguments of anyone who disagreed with you?

....

....

....

ACTIVITY 3: LOGICAL UNDERSTANDING

1. How did paraphrasing and acknowledging the logic of someone's argument affect the discussions?

....

....

HOMEWORK

Practice disagreeing agreeably.

HOMEWORK TRACKER

Who did you paraphrase?

....

....

....

....

....

....

What was the logic behind what they said?

....

....

....

....

....

....

What happened after you paraphrased what they said with an affirmation of their logic?

....

....

....

....

....

....

UNIT 2: POST-ASSESSMENT

To what extent do you agree with each statement?

1. I am a good listener.

☐ *Strongly Disagree*   ☐ *Disagree*   ☐ *Agree*   ☐ *Strongly Agree*

2. I know how to show someone that I understand them.

☐ *Strongly Disagree*   ☐ *Disagree*   ☐ *Agree*   ☐ *Strongly Agree*

3. I can show someone I understand them even if they disagree with me.

☐ *Strongly Disagree*   ☐ *Disagree*   ☐ *Agree*   ☐ *Strongly Agree*

4. I have improved my listening skills because of this learning unit.

☐ *Strongly Disagree*   ☐ *Disagree*   ☐ *Agree*   ☐ *Strongly Agree*

5. I have improved my ability to show someone that I understand them because of this learning unit.

☐ *Strongly Disagree*   ☐ *Disagree*   ☐ *Agree*   ☐ *Strongly Agree*

6. I have improved my ability to show someone I understand them even if they disagree with me.

☐ *Strongly Disagree*   ☐ *Disagree*   ☐ *Agree*   ☐ *Strongly Agree*

Complete the prompt:

7. What I learned about listening that will help me in school:

....

....

....

....

....

8. What I learned about listening that will help me in life:

....

....

....

....

....

9. What I still want to learn or experience:

....

....

....

....

....

UNIT 3: Respect

LESSON 13: ALL ABOUT RESPECT

ACTIVITY 1: OPENING QUESTIONS

1. What does respect mean to you?

....

....

....

2. How do you know when someone is giving you respect or not?

....

....

....

ACTIVITY 2: SHARED DEFINITION

1. How did your understanding and perspective of this word change after your group discussion?

....

....

....

....

ACTIVITY 3: GROUP KNOT

1. How did students demonstrate respect during the activities?

....

....

....

HOMEWORK

Notice at least one act of respect.

HOMEWORK TRACKER

Person who demonstrated respect

....

....

....

....

....

What did they do?

....

....

....

....

....

....

What happened afterwards?

....

....

....

....

....

....

LESSON 14: TREATING OTHERS WITH RESPECT

ACTIVITY 1: OPENING QUESTIONS

1. How do you want others to demonstrate respect to you?

....

....

....

2. How do you demonstrate respect to others?

....

....

....

ACTIVITY 2: TWO GOLDEN RULES

1. How can you use the "second" Golden Rule in your life?

....

....

....

....

ACTIVITY 3: CREATOR, SCULPTOR, CLAY

1. How was the "second" Golden Rule applied in this activity?

....

....

....

....

....

2. How were people respectful of each other?

....

....

....

....

....

....

....

HOMEWORK

Notice the different ways people want to be respected.

HOMEWORK TRACKER

Who did you respect in the way they wanted to be respected?

....

....

....

....

....

What did you do?

....

....

....

....

....

How did they react?

....

....

....

....

What did they feel?

....

....

....

....

What happened afterwards?

....

....

....

....

LESSON 15: INCLUSION

ACTIVITY 1: OPENING QUESTION

1. When have you ever felt included or excluded from a group?

....

....

....

ACTIVITY 2: COMMONALITIES AND DIFFERENCES

1. What was it like to learn commonalities among your classmates?

....

....

....

2. What was it like when you struggled to find something in common with someone else?

....

....

....

3. What was it like to identify the differences between your classmates?

....

....

....

....

ACTIVITY 3: JIGSAW PUZZLE

1. How will inclusion strengthen our class?

....

....

....

....

....

....

....

HOMEWORK

Take one action towards inclusion. Notice how you feel.

HOMEWORK TRACKER

What act towards inclusion did you take?

....

....

....

How did you feel?

....

....

....

What was the result?

....

....

....

LESSON 16: KINDNESS EXPERIMENT

ACTIVITY 1: OPENING QUESTION

1. What's the nicest thing you have ever done for someone?

....

....

....

2. What's the nicest thing someone did for you?

....

....

....

ACTIVITY 2: BROKEN SQUARES

1. Was it challenging to need others to fix your broken square?

....

....

....

....

2. How is this game a metaphor for life?

....

....

....

ACTIVITY 3: WHY KINDNESS?

1. What did you notice about how you felt when you did something kind?

....

....

....

2. What effect did it have on someone else?

....

....

....

....

HOMEWORK

Do three acts of kindness.

HOMEWORK TRACKER

What were your three acts of kindness?

....

....

....

How did you feel afterwards?

....

....

....

What happened after you did something kind?

....

....

....

UNIT 3: POST-ASSESSMENT

To what extent do you agree with each statement?

1. After this SEL unit on Respect, I have increased my understanding of how to show respect.

   ☐ *Strongly Disagree*   ☐ *Disagree*   ☐ *Agree*   ☐ *Strongly Agree*

2. My classmates treat each other with more respect after this SEL unit.

   ☐ *Strongly Disagree*   ☐ *Disagree*   ☐ *Agree*   ☐ *Strongly Agree*

Complete the prompt:

3. What I learned about respect that will help me in school:

   ....

   ....

   ....

   ....

   ....

4. What I learned about respect that will help me in life:

   ....

   ....

   ....

....

....

5. What I still want to learn or experience:

....

....

....

....

....

UNIT 4: Emotional Literacy

LESSON 17: CONNECTING TO FEELINGS—PART 1

ACTIVITY 1: OPENING QUESTION

1. What feelings have you had so far today?

....

....

....

ACTIVITY 2: NOTICING YOUR FEELINGS

1. What feelings did you have?

....

....

2. Did you always feel something?

....

....

3. What can you conclude about feelings after doing this activity?

....

....

ACTIVITY 3: FEELINGS CHARADES

1. What nonverbal cues were you able to detect in order to make a guess about feelings?

   ....

   ....

   ....

2. When and how is this skill useful in life?

   ....

   ....

   ....

ACTIVITY 4: FEELINGS SCENARIOS

1. What did you learn about feelings today?

   ....

   ....

HOMEWORK

Notice your feelings.

HOMEWORK TRACKER

A feeling you experienced

....

....

....

....

....

What was happening around you?

....

....

....

....

....

LESSON 18: CONNECTING TO FEELINGS—PART 2

ACTIVITY 1: OPENING QUESTION

1. What was one feeling you felt between last class and this class?

....

....

ACTIVITY 2: EMOTIONAL STACKING

1. Why might it be useful to identify the intensity of a feeling?

....

....

....

ACTIVITY 3: FEELINGS ART

1. Which feelings did you connect in this activity?

....

....

....

HOMEWORK

Notice how your feelings either went up or down in intensity and why.

HOMEWORK TRACKER

Feeling

....

....

....

....

What was happening around you?

....

....

....

....

How did your feeling change?

....

....

....

....

....

....

What was happening around you when your feeling changed?

....

....

....

....

....

....

LESSON 19: FEELINGS PRACTICE

ACTIVITY 1: OPENING QUESTION

1. How can you tell what someone is feeling?

....

....

....

ACTIVITY 2: GROUP FEELINGS SEARCH

1. What physical cues do you give to indicate how you feel?

....

....

....

2. What did you see in other students' expressions that indicated what they were feeling?

....

....

....

....

ACTIVITY 3: FOLLOW THE LEADER / FEELINGS VERSION

1. Was it difficult to copy the leader's emotional state?

....

....

....

2. Did acting out an emotion make you feel any differently?

....

....

....

ACTIVITY 4: FEELING IN A BAG

1. What did you learn about your classmates' experiences?

....

....

HOMEWORK

Notice what other people are feeling.

HOMEWORK TRACKER

Who did you observe?

....

....

....

What feeling did you guess they were having?

....

....

....

Why?

....

....

....

LESSON 20: FEELINGS EXPLORATION

ACTIVITY 1: OPENING QUESTION

1. What caused your feelings to change?

....

....

....

ACTIVITY 2: EMOTIONAL ROLLER COASTER

1. How did the student actors' emotions affect what was said?

....

....

....

2. What is it like to experience a range of emotions?

....

....

....

....

ACTIVITY 3: UNCERTAIN FEELINGS

1. What have you learned about being a feelings detective?

....

....

....

HOMEWORK

Guess what someone is feeling.

HOMEWORK TRACKER

Who was the subject of your guess?

....

....

....

....

....

Was your guess right?

....

....

....

....

....

....

What happened after you guessed their feelings?

....

....

....

....

....

....

LESSON 21: FEELINGS...NOW WHAT?

ACTIVITY 1: OPENING QUESTION

1. When have you had a strong positive or negative feeling in your life? What action did you take?

....

....

....

ACTIVITY 2: FEELINGS AND ACTION

1. When are feelings a good guide to action?

....

....

....

2. When are they not?

....

....

....

....

FEELING ACTION

SCARED- SEEK SAFETY

DISGUSTED- LET'S NOT DO THAT AGAIN

HAPPINESS- DO IT AGAIN

ACTIVITY 3: TRIGGERS

1. What did you notice about your relationship between feelings and actions?

....

....

HOMEWORK

Notice what decisions are driven by your feelings.

HOMEWORK TRACKER

When did you notice you were triggered?

....

....

....

....

....

How did you respond?

....

....

....

....

....

....

....

Did you feel in control of your actions?

....

....

....

....

....

....

....

LESSON 22: PRECISION WITH FEELINGS, THOUGHTS, AND JUDGMENTS

ACTIVITY 1: OPENING QUESTION

1. What's the difference between a feeling and a thought?

....

....

....

....

ACTIVITY 2: FEELINGS AND THOUGHTS

1. When will it be most useful for you to separate feelings from thoughts?

....

....

....

....

....

....

ACTIVITY 3: FEELINGS WITH HIDDEN JUDGMENTS

1. What is the value of expressing feelings with judgments in a different way?

....

....

....

....

ACTIVITY 4: FEELINGS AND OBSERVATIONS PRACTICE

1. When would you use feelings and observations?

....

....

....

....

HOMEWORK

Notice when people express feelings that have hidden judgments.

Try responding to a situation by expressing a feeling and observation.

HOMEWORK TRACKER

What situation did you observe?

....

....

....

....

....

What were your feelings without judgments?

....

....

....

....

....

UNIT 4: POST-ASSESSMENT

To what extent do you agree with each statement?

1. After this SEL unit, I am more connected to my feelings.

☐ *Strongly Disagree*   ☐ *Disagree*   ☐ *Agree*   ☐ *Strongly Agree*

2. After this SEL unit, I am better at noticing other people's feelings.

☐ *Strongly Disagree*   ☐ *Disagree*   ☐ *Agree*   ☐ *Strongly Agree*

3. After this SEL unit, I make good decisions when I have a strong emotional reaction.

☐ *Strongly Disagree*   ☐ *Disagree*   ☐ *Agree*   ☐ *Strongly Agree*

Complete the prompt:

4. What I learned about feelings that will help me in school:

....

....

....

....

....

....

5. What I learned about feelings that will help me in life:

....

....

....

....

....

....

6. What I still want to learn or experience:

....

....

....

....

....

....

UNIT 5: Empathy

LESSON 23: FEELINGS EMPATHY

ACTIVITY 1: OPENING QUESTION

1. What do you do or say when you want to show you understand how someone feels?

....

....

....

....

ACTIVITY 2: EMOTION MOTION

1. What did you do to show emotion?

....

....

....

....

....

....

....

ACTIVITY 3: WHAT EMPATHY ISN'T

1. How does empathy differ from other responses?

....

....

....

....

ACTIVITY 4: EMPATHY PRACTICE

1. How did it feel to receive empathy?

....

....

....

....

....

....

HOMEWORK

Give someone empathy.

HOMEWORK TRACKER

Who did you give empathy to?

....

....

....

....

....

What was the result?

....

....

....

....

....

LESSON 24: CONNECTION THROUGH TONE

ACTIVITY 1: OPENING QUESTION

1. What tone do you use when you want people to take you seriously?

....

....

ACTIVITY 2: TONAL EMPATHY

1. How does tone affect empathy?

....

....

ACTIVITY 3: TONAL EMPATHY PRACTICE

1. What did it feel like when someone connected to not only your feelings, but your tone of voice?

....

....

....

HOMEWORK

Notice what tone people use to express their feelings.

HOMEWORK TRACKER

Who did you notice?

....

....

....

....

What tone did they use?

....

....

....

....

LESSON 25: VALUES EMPATHY

ACTIVITY 1: OPENING QUESTIONS

1. Besides physical needs, what does everyone need?

....

....

ACTIVITY 2: ALL ABOUT NEEDS

1. Which need did you resonate with the most?

....

....

ACTIVITY 3: NEEDS CHARADES

1. How did you figure out the need that someone was expressing?

....

....

....

ACTIVITY 4: NEEDS EMPATHY PRACTICE

1. What was it like to receive needs empathy?

....

....

....

....

....

....

2. How did needs empathy compare to feelings empathy?

....

....

....

....

....

....

HOMEWORK

Assess what someone else is needing.

HOMEWORK TRACKER

Whose needs did you consider?

....

....

....

What did you guess they were needing?

....

....

....

Why?

....

....

....

LESSON 26: ALL ROADS LEAD TO NEEDS

ACTIVITY 1: OPENING QUESTION

1. What are you feeling and what do you need?

....

....

....

ACTIVITY 2: MET AND UNMET NEEDS

1. Do you find it useful to identify your met needs?

....

....

....

2. What did you notice about the relationship between feelings and needs?

....

....

....

....

> ARE YOU FEELING DISAPPOINTED WITH A NEED FOR RESPECT?

ACTIVITY 3: JUDGMENTS AND NEEDS

1. What is the benefit of translating judgments into needs?

....

....

....

....

ACTIVITY 4: NEEDS EMPATHY PRACTICE

1. How does knowing people are trying to have their needs met change your perception of the world?

....

....

....

HOMEWORK

Translate someone's judgments into a guess about their needs.

HOMEWORK TRACKER

Judgment you heard

....

....

....

....

....

The need behind the judgment

....

....

....

....

....

LESSON 27: EMPATHY SIMILES

ACTIVITY 1: OPENING QUESTION

1. What are your favorite similes?

....

....

ACTIVITY 2: SIMILE CHECK IN

1. Which postcard did you choose?

....

....

2. How did it represent how you felt?

....

....

3. Was this an effective way to share feelings?

....

....

ACTIVITY 3: SIMILE EMPATHY

1. What similes did you create for empathy?

....

....

....

....

ACTIVITY 4: TOOTHPICK ON BOTTLE PASS

1. Was simile empathy effective for you?

....

....

....

....

....

....

HOMEWORK

Show someone empathy by asking them about their feelings using a simile.

HOMEWORK TRACKER

Who you gave empathy to?

....

....

....

What simile empathy guess did you give?

....

....

....

What was the result?

....

....

....

UNIT 5: Post-Assessment

To what extent do you agree with each statement?

1. After this SEL unit, I am better at giving empathy.

☐ *Strongly Disagree*　　☐ *Disagree*　　☐ *Agree*　　☐ *Strongly Agree*

2. I understand multiple ways of giving empathy.

☐ *Strongly Disagree*　　☐ *Disagree*　　☐ *Agree*　　☐ *Strongly Agree*

3. Practicing empathy has improved my life.

☐ *Strongly Disagree*　　☐ *Disagree*　　☐ *Agree*　　☐ *Strongly Agree*

Complete the prompt:

4. What I learned about empathy that will help me in school:

....

....

....

....

....

....

5. What I learned about empathy that will help me in life:

....

....

....

....

....

....

6. What I still want to learn or experience:

....

....

....

....

....

....

UNIT 6: Communication

LESSON 28: EFFECTIVE AND INEFFECTIVE COMMUNICATION

ACTIVITY 1: OPENING QUESTION

1. When were you successful with communication and when were you unsuccessful?

....

....

ACTIVITY 2: QUICK LOOK

1. What did you learn about effective communication?

....

....

....

ACTIVITY 3: SHARED DEFINITION

1. How have your definition and understanding of communication changed after this activity?

....

....

ACTIVITY 4: Lost at Sea

1. Did you experience effective or ineffective communication today?

....

....

HOMEWORK

Notice examples of effective and ineffective communication in your life.

HOMEWORK TRACKER

When did you notice effective communication?

....

....

....

....

....

What made the communication work?

....

....

....

....

When did you notice ineffective communication?

....

....

....

....

What was the problem?

....

....

....

....

LESSON 29: PARAPHRASE REQUEST

ACTIVITY 1: OPENING QUESTION

1. How can you make sure someone else understands what you said?

....

....

....

....

....

ACTIVITY 2: PARAPHRASE REQUEST

1. How much more clarity was gained once you requested other students to paraphrase what they heard them say?

CAN YOU TELL ME WHAT YOU HEARD ME SAY?

....

....

....

....

....

....

ACTIVITY 3: DIALOGUE WITH PARAPHRASE REQUEST

1. When is it appropriate to request someone to paraphrase what you said?

....

....

....

HOMEWORK

Ask one person, but not an adult, to share what they heard you say as politely as possible.

HOMEWORK TRACKER

What did you say?

....

....

....

....

What did the other person hear?

....

....

....

....

....

....

Did the request for paraphrasing help?

....

....

....

....

....

....

LESSON 30: COMMUNICATION STYLES

ACTIVITY 1: OPENING QUESTION

1. Do you consider yourself a passive, assertive, or aggressive person? Why?

....

....

....

....

....

ACTIVITY 2: COMMUNICATION STYLE ASSESSMENT

1. What did you learn about each communication style?

....

....

....

....

....

....

....

ACTIVITY 3: RESTING RULERS

1. What is your dominant communication style?

....

....

....

....

HOMEWORK

Notice the communication styles of different people.

HOMEWORK TRACKER

Who did you notice?

....

....

....

....

What communication style did they demonstrate?

....

....

....

....

....

....

Why did you think this?

....

....

....

....

....

....

LESSON 31: COMMUNICATION TOOLS

ACTIVITY 1: OPENING QUESTION

1. When have you had an argument that escalated or became more heated?

....

....

....

2. What happened?

....

....

....

ACTIVITY 2: OBSERVATION AND JUDGMENT

1. How does using observational language assist clear communication?

....

....

....

ACTIVITY 3: REQUESTS AND DEMANDS

1. When is it appropriate to make a request and when is it appropriate to make a demand?

....

....

....

....

ACTIVITY 4: OBSERVATION AND REQUEST PRACTICE

1. How did using observations and requests influence communication?

....

....

....

....

....

HOMEWORK

Use observational language and requests when you have a conflict.

HOMEWORK TRACKER

What was the conflict?

....

....

....

....

....

What observational language did you use?

....

....

....

....

....

What did you request?

....

....

....

....

....

....

....

What was the result?

....

....

....

....

....

....

....

LESSON 32: "I" STATEMENT

ACTIVITY 1: OPENING QUESTION

1. When you are upset, how can you express yourself assertively without being either passive or aggressive?

....

....

ACTIVITY 2: "I" STATEMENT PRACTICE

1. What are the advantages and disadvantages of using an "I" statement?

I FEEL _____ WHEN YOU_____
BECAUSE _____. CAN YOU _____?

....

....

....

ACTIVITY 3: "I" STATEMENT ROLE PLAY

1. Do you prefer Observation and Requests or "I" statements?

....

....

HOMEWORK

Try to use an "I" statement when someone bothers you.

HOMEWORK TRACKER

What "I" statement did you use?

....

....

....

....

What was the result?

....

....

....

....

LESSON 33: INTENTION

ACTIVITY 1: OPENING QUESTION

1. How do you react when someone wants to prove you wrong?

....

....

....

....

....

ACTIVITY 2: BEING RIGHT

1. How does intention affect conversation?

THAT'S HOW IT IS AND I'M RIGHT!

....

....

....

....

....

....

....

ACTIVITY 3: Truth and Communication

1. What do you know to be true that may only be an incomplete depiction of a greater truth?

....

....

....

....

....

ACTIVITY 4: Intention Practice

1. What did you learn about intention and results?

....

....

....

....

HOMEWORK

Notice your intention in your conversations.

HOMEWORK TRACKER

Your intention before a conversation

....

....

....

....

....

What was the conversation like?

....

....

....

....

....

UNIT 6: Post-Assessment

To what extent do you agree with each statement?

1. I improved my communication skills.

☐ *Strongly Disagree*   ☐ *Disagree*   ☐ *Agree*   ☐ *Strongly Agree*

2. I understand the importance of precise language.

☐ *Strongly Disagree*   ☐ *Disagree*   ☐ *Agree*   ☐ *Strongly Agree*

3. I have tools to de-escalate conflict.

☐ *Strongly Disagree*   ☐ *Disagree*   ☐ *Agree*   ☐ *Strongly Agree*

Complete the prompt:

4. What I learned about communication that will help me in school:

....

....

....

....

....

5. What I learned about communication that will help me in life:

....

....

....

....

....

6. What I still want to learn or experience:

....

....

....

....

....

UNIT 7: Integrity

LESSON 34: MORALITY

ACTIVITY 1: OPENING QUESTION

1. When in your life did you have to make a tough decision between right and wrong? What did you choose? Why?

....

....

....

....

....

ACTIVITY 2: RIGHT AND WRONG

1. What are the advantages and disadvantages of thinking about what is right and wrong?

DID YOU JUST SAY THAT TO MAKE YOURSELF LOOK GOOD?

....

....

....

....

....

....

ACTIVITY 3: HONESTY

1. What is your relationship with honesty?

....

....

....

....

....

ACTIVITY 4: WHAT WOULD YOU DO?

1. What did you find interesting about the discussion about right and wrong?

....

....

....

....

....

HOMEWORK

Notice when people act with integrity.

HOMEWORK TRACKER

What act of integrity or lack of integrity did you witness?

....

....

....

....

....

What was the result?

....

....

....

....

....

LESSON 35: RULES

ACTIVITY 1: OPENING QUESTION

1. What are some good and bad rules in school, at home, and in the world?

....

....

ACTIVITY 2: RULES DISCUSSION

1. What is your relationship with rules?

....

....

....

ACTIVITY 3: WITH AND WITHOUT RULES

1. What happens when rules are broken?

....

....

....

ACTIVITY 4: PULSE

1. What is the relationship between integrity and rules?

....

....

....

HOMEWORK

Notice when people follow and don't follow rules.

HOMEWORK TRACKER

Rule

....

....

....

....

....

Followed or broken?

....

....

....

....

....

....

....

What was the result?

....

....

....

....

....

....

....

LESSON 36: KEEPING YOUR WORD

ACTIVITY 1: OPENING QUESTION

1. When did you experience someone who did what they said they were going to do or when someone did not do what they said they were going to do?

....

....

....

....

ACTIVITY 2: YOUR WORD

1. Why is keeping your word important?

....

....

....

....

....

ACTIVITY 3: TRUST WALK

1. How can you be trustworthy?

....

....

....

....

....

....

ACTIVITY 4: MAKING THINGS RIGHT

1. What's the relationship between trust and giving your word?

....

....

....

....

HOMEWORK

Next time you make a promise/give your word to do something, note whether you keep it.

HOMEWORK TRACKER

What did you say you would do?

....

....

....

....

....

What was the result?

....

....

....

....

....

LESSON 37: EXCUSES

ACTIVITY 1: OPENING QUESTION

1. What is the worst excuse you have ever heard?

....

....

ACTIVITY 2: GOOD AND BAD EXCUSES

1. Why is it important to distinguish between a good and bad excuse?

....

....

....

....

ACTIVITY 3: CREATIVE SOLUTIONS

1. How does a creative solution show integrity?

....

....

ACTIVITY 4: Choices

1. How do excuses hinder effectiveness?

....

....

....

....

....

2. What would taking responsibility look like in your life?

....

....

....

....

....

HOMEWORK

Notice when you make an excuse, and instead take responsibility for the situation.

HOMEWORK TRACKER

What went wrong?

....

....

....

....

....

What was the excuse?

....

....

....

....

....

What does responsibility look like?

....

....

....

....

....

....

What would be a creative solution?

....

....

....

....

....

....

LESSON 38: GROUP INTEGRITY

ACTIVITY 1: OPENING QUESTION

1. How is the group affected when one person doesn't act with integrity?

....

....

ACTIVITY 2: ROPE SHAPES

1. How did everyone's integrity affect the success of the group?

....

....

....

....

ACTIVITY 3: OCTOPUS BRAIN

1. What was it like to share leadership?

....

....

2. What's the relationship between leading, following, and acting with integrity?

....

....

....

....

ACTIVITY 4: PAPER CLIP CHAIN

1. What is the best way to create group integrity?

....

....

....

....

....

....

....

HOMEWORK

Notice how and why groups work effectively or ineffectively.

HOMEWORK TRACKER

Effective group action

....

....

....

....

....

Why was the group effective?

....

....

....

....

....

Ineffective group action

....

....

....

....

....

....

....

Why was the group ineffective?

....

....

....

....

....

....

UNIT 7: Post-Assessment

To what extent do you agree with each statement?

1. I value the importance of integrity.

☐ *Strongly Disagree*   ☐ *Disagree*   ☐ *Agree*   ☐ *Strongly Agree*

2. I value rules.

☐ *Strongly Disagree*   ☐ *Disagree*   ☐ *Agree*   ☐ *Strongly Agree*

3. I value the importance of keeping your word.

☐ *Strongly Disagree*   ☐ *Disagree*   ☐ *Agree*   ☐ *Strongly Agree*

4. I have a stronger relationship with integrity after this unit.

☐ *Strongly Disagree*   ☐ *Disagree*   ☐ *Agree*   ☐ *Strongly Agree*

Complete the prompt:

5. What I learned about integrity that will help me in school:

....

....

....

....

....

6. What I learned about integrity that will help me in life:

....

....

....

....

....

7. What I still want to learn or experience:

....

....

....

....

....

UNIT 8: MINDFULNESS

LESSON 39: BREATH

ACTIVITY 1: OPENING QUESTION

1. When do you notice your breath?

....

....

ACTIVITY 2: BREATHING TECHNIQUES

1. How do your body and mind feel after these activities?

....

....

....

....

ACTIVITY 3: BREATH AND FOCUS

1. What impact did mindful breathing have on you?

....

....

HOMEWORK

Stop and just notice your breath for 1 min. Notice what effect this has on you.

HOMEWORK TRACKER

What was it like to notice your breath?

....

....

....

....

What happened afterwards?

....

....

....

....

LESSON 40: SENSORY MINDFULNESS

ACTIVITY 1: OPENING QUESTION

1. How do you stay present in the moment?

....

....

....

....

....

ACTIVITY 2: FIVE SENSES MINDFULNESS

1. Which sensory exploration helped you feel more present?

....

....

....

....

....

....

....

ACTIVITY 3: RICE AND BEANS COUNT

1. What did you learn about being present?

....

....

....

HOMEWORK

For 1 minute, stop and focus on the present moment using one of your 5 senses.

HOMEWORK TRACKER

What sense did you use?

....

....

....

....

How did it feel?

....

....

....

....

....

....

....

What happened after?

....

....

....

....

....

....

....

LESSON 41: SELF-TALK

ACTIVITY 1: OPENING QUESTION

1. What topics do you think or daydream about most often?

....

....

ACTIVITY 2: NOTICING YOUR THINKING

1. What did you notice about your thoughts?

....

....

....

....

ACTIVITY 3: PROBLEM SOLVING SELF-TALK

1. What type of thoughts did you become aware of?

....

....

HOMEWORK

Bring awareness to your thinking throughout the day.

HOMEWORK TRACKER

What did you think about?

....

....

....

....

Did it become helpful to you to notice your thinking?

....

....

....

....

LESSON 42: MINDFULNESS...NOW WHAT?

ACTIVITY 1: OPENING QUESTION

1. How can you use your mindfulness skills?

   ....

   ....

   ....

ACTIVITY 2: FOCUS

1. How does focus affect what we see and notice?

   ....

   ....

   ....

2. How can we use this knowledge to improve our lives?

   ....

   ....

   ....

   ....

ACTIVITY 3: Two Circles

1. How can you apply the Lesson from "Two Wolves" to your life?

....

....

....

....

ACTIVITY 4: Tangrams

1. How did your awareness of your thoughts influence your productivity?

....

....

....

....

....

HOMEWORK

Notice what you are thinking about as you approach an obstacle.

HOMEWORK TRACKER

Obstacle

....

....

....

What thoughts did you notice?

....

....

....

How did you use the awareness of your thoughts to overcome the obstacle?

....

....

....

UNIT 8: POST-ASSESSMENT

To what extent do you agree with each statement?

1. I can use the awareness of my breath to be more present.

☐ *Strongly Disagree*   ☐ *Disagree*   ☐ *Agree*   ☐ *Strongly Agree*

2. I can use my sensory experiences to be more present.

☐ *Strongly Disagree*   ☐ *Disagree*   ☐ *Agree*   ☐ *Strongly Agree*

3. I am more aware of my thoughts.

☐ *Strongly Disagree*   ☐ *Disagree*   ☐ *Agree*   ☐ *Strongly Agree*

4. I can use the awareness of my thoughts to make better decisions.

☐ *Strongly Disagree*   ☐ *Disagree*   ☐ *Agree*   ☐ *Strongly Agree*

Complete the prompt:

5. What I learned about mindfulness that will help me in school:

....

....

....

....

....

6. What I learned about mindfulness that will help me in life:

....

....

....

....

....

7. What I still want to learn or experience:

....

....

....

....

....

UNIT 9: Goal Setting

LESSON 43: STARTING WITH GOALS

ACTIVITY 1: OPENING QUESTION

1. What is a goal you had that you were able to achieve?

....

....

ACTIVITY 2: GOAL PLANNING

1. What does it feel like to think about all the things you want in life?

....

....

....

....

ACTIVITY 3: SMART GOALS

1. What did you learn about achieving a goal?

....

....

HOMEWORK

Take one action towards your goal.

HOMEWORK TRACKER

Goal

....

....

....

....

Action taken

....

....

....

....

LESSON 44: Step by Step

ACTIVITY 1: Opening Question

1. Did you make progress towards your goal? Why or why not?

....

....

ACTIVITY 2: Step by Step Map

1. What is the value of breaking up a goal into steps?

....

....

....

....

ACTIVITY 3: Juggling Scarves

1. What steps will you take between now and next class to achieve your goal?

....

....

HOMEWORK

Take a few steps towards your goal.

HOMEWORK TRACKER

Goal

....

....

....

....

Steps taken

....

....

....

....

LESSON 45: CREATIVE SOLUTIONS

ACTIVITY 1: OPENING QUESTION

1. What successes and what obstacles did you encounter trying to achieve your goal?

....

....

....

ACTIVITY 2: TRAFFIC JAM

1. What did you learn about solving problems?

....

....

....

ACTIVITY 3: BLANKET FLIP

1. How can you apply what you learned about solving problems to other situations in life?

....

....

....

....

ACTIVITY 4: OBSTACLES AND CREATIVE SOLUTIONS

1. How can creative solutions help you in your life?

....

....

....

....

HOMEWORK

Notice how you react to an obstacle and seek a creative solution.

HOMEWORK TRACKER

Obstacle

....

....

....

....

....

Creative solution

....

....

....

....

....

LESSON 46: INCREASING THE POSSIBILITY FOR SUCCESS

ACTIVITY 1: OPENING QUESTION

1. How do you motivate yourself?

....

....

....

....

....

ACTIVITY 2: MOTIVATION AND INSPIRATION

1. What are the best ways for you to increase your motivation and decrease your distractions?

....

....

....

....

....

ACTIVITY 3: CELEBRATIONS

1. What celebrations will you plan during or after you achieve your goal?

....

....

....

....

ACTIVITY 4: FEATHER BALANCING

1. What helped and what did not help your feather balancing attempts?

....

....

....

....

....

HOMEWORK

Change your environment to increase the possibility of achieving your goal.

HOMEWORK TRACKER

Goal

....

....

....

....

....

How I increased the likelihood of success

....

....

....

....

....

UNIT 9: POST-ASSESSMENT

To what extent do you agree with each statement?

1. I am aware of my goals.

☐ *Strongly Disagree*   ☐ *Disagree*   ☐ *Agree*   ☐ *Strongly Agree*

2. I know how to measure my progress towards my goals.

☐ *Strongly Disagree*   ☐ *Disagree*   ☐ *Agree*   ☐ *Strongly Agree*

3. I know how to increase the likelihood of achieving my goal.

☐ *Strongly Disagree*   ☐ *Disagree*   ☐ *Agree*   ☐ *Strongly Agree*

Complete the prompt:

4. What I learned about goals that will help me in school:

....

....

....

....

....

5. What I learned about goals that will help me in life:

....

....

....

....

....

6. What I still want to learn or experience:

....

....

....

....

....

UNIT 10: RESILIENCE

BUZZZ!!!

LESSON 47: BOUNCING BACK

ACTIVITY 1: OPENING QUESTION

1. How do you deal with struggle?

....

....

....

ACTIVITY 2: MAZE

1. What did you learn about learning from mistakes?

....

....

....

....

....

BUZZZ!!!

HOMEWORK

Note how you handle difficulty.

HOMEWORK TRACKER

Mistake

....

....

....

....

....

Response

....

....

....

....

....

LESSON 48: GROWTH MINDSET

ACTIVITY 1: OPENING QUESTIONS

1. What percentage of success is due to talent?

....

....

....

2. What percentage is due to effort?

....

....

....

ACTIVITY 2: GROWTH MINDSET VS. FIXED MINDSET

1. How can a growth mindset benefit you?

....

....

....

....

....

ACTIVITY 3: Growth Mindset Practice

1. How can a growth mindset help you learn?

....

....

....

HOMEWORK

Notice when you are thinking with a growth mindset or a fixed mindset.

HOMEWORK TRACKER

Learning tasks

....

....

....

....

Thoughts

....

....

....

....

....

....

....

Growth mindset or Fixed mindset

....

....

....

....

....

....

LESSON 49: BELIEFS

ACTIVITY 1: OPENING QUESTION

1. What do people need to believe to be successful?

....

....

....

ACTIVITY 2: BELIEFS IN ACTION

1. How did your beliefs about what was possible affect your action?

....

....

....

2. How did your partner's beliefs/ideas about success impact your actions and results?

....

....

....

....

ACTIVITY 3: WIRE PUZZLES

1. How do you create hope when things seem impossible?

....

....

....

HOMEWORK

Notice what you believe about a task as you do it.

HOMEWORK TRACKER

Task

....

....

....

....

....

Belief

....

....

....

....

....

....

....

Result

....

....

....

....

....

....

LESSON 50: PRACTICE

ACTIVITY 1: OPENING QUESTION

1. What is your relationship with practice?

....

....

....

ACTIVITY 2: NUMBERS SEARCH

1. What did you learn about the value of repeating an activity?

....

....

....

ACTIVITY 3: RIVER CROSSING

1. What are the benefits of practice?

....

....

....

....

2. What makes practice difficult?

....

....

....

HOMEWORK

Notice your thinking as you practice a skill.

HOMEWORK TRACKER

Skill

....

....

....

....

Practice

....

....

....

....

....

....

....

Result

....

....

....

....

....

....

....

UNIT 10: POST-ASSESSMENT

To what extent do you agree with each statement?

1. I know how to bounce back after failure.

☐ *Strongly Disagree*   ☐ *Disagree*   ☐ *Agree*   ☐ *Strongly Agree*

2. I understand the value of a growth mindset.

☐ *Strongly Disagree*   ☐ *Disagree*   ☐ *Agree*   ☐ *Strongly Agree*

3. I am aware of my beliefs.

☐ *Strongly Disagree*   ☐ *Disagree*   ☐ *Agree*   ☐ *Strongly Agree*

4. I appreciate the value of practice.

☐ *Strongly Disagree*   ☐ *Disagree*   ☐ *Agree*   ☐ *Strongly Agree*

Complete the prompt:

5. What I learned about resilience that will help me in school:

....

....

....

....

....

6. What I learned about resilience that will help me in life:

....

....

....

....

....

7. What I still want to learn or experience:

....

....

....

....

....

SUCCESS TRACKER QUESTIONNAIRE

1. What do I want?

....

....

2. What do I need?

....

....

3. What specific goal do I want to achieve?

....

....

4. What SEL skills do I want to practice?

....

....

5. What are the challenges?

....

....

6. What have other people done to achieve the same goal?

....

....

7. What strategies will help me achieve what I want or need?

....

....

8. How do I acknowledge or celebrate success?

....

....

9. What can I handle challenges?

....

....

10. What support do I need?

....

....

11. Who can give me feedback and support?

....

....

12. How do I measure success?

....

....

SAMPLE GOALS

- Improve study habits
- Be more positive
- Manage anger
- Learn to play an instrument
- Improve sleep habits
- Improve relationship with a sibling
- Increase energy
- Get in less trouble at school
- Spend less time on social media

- Read more
- Get better at video games
- Manage stress more effectively
- Improve eating habits
- Improve relationships with friends
- Practice a skill
- Be nicer to others
- Be more physically active
- Increase creativity

....

....

....

....

....

SAMPLE SEL SKILLS

- Identifying emotions
- Emotional regulation
- Thought regulation
- Self-confidence
- Recognizing strengths and challenges
- Perspective-taking
- Conflict de-escalation
- Social engagement
- Problem solving
- Values identification
- Resilience
- Acceptance
- Self-connection
- Body-mind awareness
- Responsible decision making
- Impulse control

- Organizational skills
- Time management
- Stress management
- Goal setting
- Perseverance
- Self-discipline
- Intrinsic motivation
- Empathy
- Respect for self and others
- Communication
- Teamwork
- Relationship-building
- Problem-solving
- Trigger identification
- Self-awareness
- Social awareness
- Curiosity

SAMPLE STRATEGIES

- Positive self-talk
- Set SMART goals
- Think before acting
- Breathing techniques to control impulses
- Use a planner
- Practice asking open-ended questions
- Set up environment to decrease distractions
- Create pro/con list
- Identify what you can control and what you can't
- Practice disagreeing respectfully
- Create a trigger and alternative action list

- Refer to a Feeling/Needs/Values list
- Complete tasks with others
- List opportunities for taking responsibility
- Peer/buddy check-in
- Notice body reactions
- Divide overwhelming task into small steps
- Identify empowering beliefs
- Replace cognitive distortions
- I-statements
- Observational language
- Seeking and offering help when needed

....

....

....

....

....

SAMPLE ASSESSMENT

1. Self-Assessment success scale (from 1–4)

   A I got a 4 today because I was nice to all of my classmate.

   B I got a 2 today because I completed some of my homework, but not all of it.

2. What I did well and what I can improve upon

   A I practiced dribbling for 20 minutes. To improve, I can do 30 minutes next time.

   B I thought about what to do before doing it but I can still improve on my decisions.

3. Checklist

   A Yes, I took 5 calm breaths when I was upset.

   B Yes, I did 10 minutes of exercise today.

SUCCESS TRACKER 1

Name .... Goal ....

SEL Skills .... Strategies ....

Support Team members ....

Date	What Happened	Assessment	Next Steps

SUCCESS TRACKER 2

Name .... **Goal** ....

SEL Skills .... **Strategies** ....

Support Team members ....

Date	What Happened	Assessment	Next Steps

SUCCESS TRACKER 3

Name .... Goal ....

SEL Skills .... Strategies ....

Support Team members ....

Date	What Happened	Assessment	Next Steps

SUCCESS TRACKER 4

Name .... Goal ....

SEL Skills .... Strategies ....

Support Team members ....

Date	What Happened	Assessment	Next Steps

SUCCESS TRACKER 5

Name .... Goal ....

SEL Skills .... Strategies ....

Support Team members ....

Date	What Happened	Assessment	Next Steps

OTHER BOOKS BY DAVID PARIS

100 Great Questions for Deep Conversations

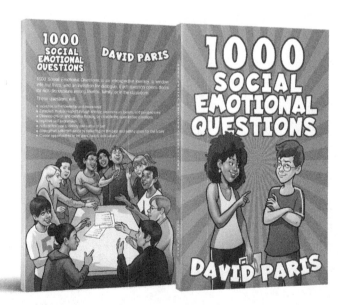

1000 Social Emotional Questions

ABOUT THE AUTHOR

David Paris is an educational consultant and has 30 years of experience teaching in NYC public schools. He is the author of 14 books, he is a group facilitator of Non-Violent Communication (NYCNVC.ORG) and a trainer with Alternative to Violence Program (AVPUSA.Org). David is also a seven-time acrobatic dance champion, co-director of Paradizo Dance, and was a finalist on America's Got Talent.

DavidParisBooks.com
SELLifeSkills.com
ParadizoDance.com

Made in United States
North Haven, CT
21 September 2023

41825207R00111